Microbursts

An Anthology of the Quabbin Writers Salon

Picaflor Press

Visit our website at:
http:/picaflorpress.weebly.com

ISBN-13: 978-0692946619 (Picaflor Press)
ISBN-10: 0692946616

Table of Contents

MICROBURSTS

"Sudden downward bursts of wind from the base of a thunderstorm, convergence occurs along the leading edge with...insects and arthropods swept along by prevailing winds, making them good indicators of outflow boundaries."
(Wikipedia)

I Don't Know What the Wooly Bear Knows

Jane McPhetres Johnson

*10-8-14: ...residents of Easthampton, MA
living at the base of Mount Tom were
awakened by the roar of trees snapping by
the thousands as a microburst packing 100-
mph winds came crashing down at the
western base of the mountain.*

Microbursts
are the worst
short on size
short on time
long on surprise.

Who knew?
Chicken Little who
stews, clucks, and
a mile-wide
chunk of sky
a cold plug of air
drops and hits the
ground running 100
or 200 miles an hour
led by an edge of
dust, spiders, bugs
feast for a hen
this outflow in
just a minute
uproots tall trees
lifts roofs and trucks

flips the switch
gives a nod and
up the chimney
we go. Who?
Who knows!

Marianne Gambaro

The Lupines of Ushuaia

in January for God's sake
almost at the bottom of the earth

improbable purples, pinks, blues, magentas
oblivious to steely sea or leaden mountains

prized specimen of Yankee gardeners
or riotous wild children running unbridled on northern hillsides

in May, early June perhaps
but never in January

turning the planet upside down
almost at its God forsaken bottom

what seeds from above earth's belt found their way here
what hubris or optimism marked their sowing
what lust their fecundity

D. Dina Friedman

Consider the Turnip...

its roots still trying to clasp the earth, its sharp
whiny taste like the conversation I heard
between two women on a Boston bus,
complaining their lives were going nowhere.

You can smell the turnip, even cold.
It's worse under fire. If I were three
I could ask without embarrassment
why the roots were purple. My husband

tried to sneak a turnip
into the pumpkin soup, but it stuck out
despite the blending. Just like intersectionality
turnips demand attention.

Touch the turnip. It's cold and clammy
like a damp refrigerator. It's the only vegetable
left in the refrigerator, and we have to eat it
because it's winter, as if winter isn't hard enough.

Can't we send the turnip on roller skates
down the puddly ice into oblivion?
Unlike the turnip, my skin shrivels
at the first sight of snow.

But like the turnip, my roots
turn purple to fight the darkness.

Maureen Solomon

I Don't Know What the Wooly Bear Knows

But the world is turning away from the sun
even though the lawn is unnaturally green
and roses are blooming on the fence
knowledge of winter casts its peculiar light
over fields where shadows fall
sooner and longer each day.

Walking down the road yesterday I stepped
over an all-black wooly bear, did not pause
to pick it up or look closely at how
darkness covered its whole body.

Folklore cast its own
chill in me, what does the wooly bear know
of climate and its changes?

Ice melting at the north pole
rocks the earth with ferocity, spawning
new weather, hotter summers, more rain here
less rain there restricting the food supply
my worries mount up as I walk along the
road where leaves fall as they have always done.

Where snow may fall too soon, damaging trees
where elderly ladies live in old houses, their shades down
where sounds of August frogs diminish, cicadas
sing less and less, where next year's Mullein is
already planting itself, and where a black wooly bear
inches himself like a warning into the woods.

Eileen P. Kennedy

Spring Song

Where were you when November flowed into infinity on the cold
flesh of a moon?
Autumn with phoneme blossoms
destined to die in the winter
Suicidally giving over
to the bleak soil
of nutrient allegory.

Warm barefoot beach days sing a child's lullaby.
Nursery rhymes and ice cream trucks create a tune.
Resting in dust balls,
waiting my return,
they compose a geography of incubating words
a dialect not yet formed.

Now, charmed by the muses
ordering the grammar of grey ground
rain rhythm rainbows regrouped,
there is a new tongue for the landscape
hearkening to the peeper's roar
looking to demarcate the syntax of the sun.

Marianne Gambaro

Last Light Rondeau

The oak is last to kiss the sun goodnight
as mockingbird and robin pause in flight
in highmost branches, warmed by sunset's glow,
drenched in gold while others sleep in shadow,
they sing their paeans to receding light.

Avian guests know well this daily rite,
a function of the tree's majestic height.
As surely as the morning's sun will follow
the oak is last to kiss the sun goodnight.

But nothing stops the sun's retreat despite
the oak's primacy and apparent might.
As darkness covers field and pond and meadow
and every living being that dwells below,
the birds resign, fall silent and alight.
The oak at last can kiss the sun goodnight.

Jane McPhetres Johnson

Dry
Upon being prescribed artificial tears in Sheridan, Wyoming

It's always been dry here.
Bones of the bison
share the sterile sand
with dinosaurs.
Our ancestors are saved,
trees turned to stone,
weeds kept.
Our love a storm of dust,
nobody cries here.
Nobody can.

D. Dina Friedman

Some Day

we will know for sure we are as alone
as the grass, the river, the cat

curled into itself in the morning sun
who knows how to be alone, in ways we don't

just as the river has found a way to be itself
without questioning.

And the mountains, the poor goats
milked for cheese, they have learned to be alone.

The wind, too, has no song of community.
It laughs as we hold hands, or try to paddle out of eddies.

Some day we'll be able to live
in our own skin, rejoice

in the company of breath
and the million cells that speak our secret words.

When the Wind Ends

Maureen Solomon

Friends

It isn't the secrets, tiny dark pockets
couched inside us, that matter. Have as many
secrets as you like. That isn't what counts
if you are counting.

It could never be the number of times
we dine together in little Chinese restaurants
or in coffee shops after midnight. Quantity
doesn't enter into it, perhaps it might help.

Nor the number of other friends you have.
I bless you and pray that you have all the friends
you need in this world. I am not jealous of your
heart, your time, your words, your waistline.

Friendship lies in a simple event that happens
when we meet. Like two doors that open together
and all the people pass through to the dance floor.
Our doors open and we pass through together.

Friendship is a sharing of space as if you are
standing below my ladder and holding it so
that I will not fall as I reach for the stars. As if
it mattered to you whether I fall or not.

Eileen P. Kennedy

Summer Reunion

Remember the reservoir?
A surface stretching from
island to brown stone shore.

Strands of algae and water lilies. Our
paddles dipping and slicing streams of
water and reed pulls.

A sly white egret flies
indifferent to our chatter
without caw or concern.

Soft swims in clear water to
allay sweat on
arms and legs.

Aching abs bathing in the sun
pulling to the next beach,
our prows high on the sand.

Late afternoon we rest,
sitting close on shore,
quiet now from our labors.

How many summers of paddling
hold our aging alliance together?
Waters rise from the dam's release.

Kathryn Holzman

Dog Days

My kitchen is redolent with herbs. I'm knee deep in preservation, surrounded by carrots, cucumbers and squash. Greens of all varieties, strawberries, radishes, and turnips. Three melons last week. Today, twenty-five tomatoes. A weekly task list dictated by my farm share, shaped by insect infestations and blight, rainfall totals.

At my feet, my dog Skylar is wasting away. She smells of old dog and is not uncomfortable. As long as she does not let me out of her sight, she is content. Left alone she will howl and howl.

While I chop, my husband, Ira, is helping our neighbor band birds. Every August, before the male ruby-throated hummingbirds depart for points South, Ira and Roger spend an afternoon counting, measuring and banding the local hummingbird colony. The men hang a feeder filled with sugar water in a birdcage, its door held open by a string which Ira grasps. When a bird enters, hungrily sucking sugar water to fatten up for his long journey south, Ira lowers the door.

Roger knows just how to handle the tiny birds. He checks for prior banding, measures the wings and beaks. Ira takes notes. Often the bird is repeat business, a frequent traveler. They make a note of which years he has been sighted, changes in his appearance.

How small my culinary efforts seem in light of a miniscule bird, barely larger than a butterfly about to make the journey to Florida, Texas or Mexico. As my tomatoes simmer, Roger gives the final bird a reward of nectar and opens his palm. With a flutter of wings, his subject flies off into the August sky. I want to tag Skylar and wait for him to return to me.

Rogers's wife Beth is away on business. She does marketing for a large pharmaceutical company and flies all over the world to gauge markets. Roger and Beth chose not to have children. When Beth is home, we often hear their arguments over the fence; they have knock-down drag-out fights which culminate in tears and amorous evenings in their backyard Jacuzzi.

I am expecting my second child. My first, Sam, is a happy toddler with his father's easy joy. Last night Ira practiced catching hummingbirds with him, showing him how to hold the bird in his small hand. They made a model out of green Legos and Sam held his precious cargo so tenderly that it brought tears to my eyes. I want to give him everything. I don't want him to see Skylar die.

Maybe it's the hormones. I have been remembering my mother sprawled out drunk on the bathroom floor one summer during my college vacation. A contentious summer. My mother, a corporate lawyer, lived to prove her worth. My brother and I were a reflection of her, our report cards her measure. She spent that summer enumerating my many shortfalls: my mediocre grades, my poor choice of major, my weight gain, my inability to find a proper boyfriend.

I tried it once. Drinking enough vodka that I didn't feel anything. It didn't work.

"At least I will never be like you," I screamed, slamming the door. Out of there for good.

"Don't expect me to pay your tuition next year." She yelled after me.

That's when I flew away. I was officially a college dropout, my mother's worst nightmare.

It would be years before I found another relationship with as much intensity as I had with my mother. Ira and I wear kid gloves, even now. We have vowed to be careful with each other.

I chop vegetables. My pantry is almost full. At the end of the day, after putting away his gear, Roger joins us on our deck looking out into the woods over glasses of Chardonnay. He describes the thrill of the hummingbird's heart throbbing in his palm. As we eat overflowing bowls of salad full of fresh farm greens, we identify bird calls: the jays' screech, the thrushes' waterfall. Sam searches for butterflies in the fields, telling our cat about the day's adventure. He is already synthesizing the experience, making it his own.

The end of summer is in sight.

Roger's phone rings and he walks to the edge of the field to answer it. When Beth is away, Roger is calmer. He visits often and throws sticks for Skylar. But he keeps his phone close, his lifeline to his wife. Beth is flying home from Thailand tonight.

Roger's face is pale when he returns.

"What's up?" Ira asks, carefully. We assume that they have had another argument and are ready to sympathize as always. We are old hands at this. Later we analyze. We are voyeurs of their passion, borrowing the intensity without the pain.

"It's gone." I can almost not hear him. As if he lacks the strength to form the words. I look over at Sam protectively, watch to be sure Skylar is still breathing.

"What's gone?" Ira gets up and puts an arm around his friend.

"Her plane. It just disappeared off the radar screen."

Ira stands there with his hands open, entreating. These things don't happen. He is a scientist waiting for a logical explanation. We listen intently, but all we can hear is the breeze in the trees and the distant gurgle of the stream. I take Sam's hand. Skylar is stretched out on the deck, his ribs rising and falling faintly. We walk into the lighted house and I look back at the two men and the old dog in the darkness. The sun goes down early these days.

My mother and I talk once a month now, long distance. She asks about my son, but makes no effort to visit. I post photos on Snapfish but she seldom comments on them. She does not understand why I would want to live in the country. "What do you do all day alone at home?" she asks. I describe the little things, pushing my son on a rope swing, watching him do his first puzzles, baking pies with fruit we have picked during the afternoon's walk.

Now I think they will find the plane.

Ira and Roger have gone to his study to call the airlines. I hear CNN in the background. The newscaster is describing the routine flight, the experienced pilot who had signed off nonchalantly as he exited Thailand's airspace at nightfall. There was no indication that anything was wrong, they repeat. The TV screen flashes in the dark room. I listen to Roger sob, hear Ira comforting him, his voice soft and gentle.

The plane disappeared with 245 passengers aboard.

"Do you remember when I taught you how to drive?" My mother asked me last month. She reminded me that she was the parent with enough patience to hold her breath when I turned too sharply, landing on our carefully manicured front lawn. She said we laughed about it later, saying that if we had driven into the living room we could have announced "We're home!" I remember her tight-lipped, the guttural noises in her throat when I stopped too quickly. How she braced herself against the dashboard.

She says she wants to be present for the baby's birth.

It occurs to me that we all reinvent our past.

More foolishly, we all pretend to control the future.

My baby kicks. I hope it's a girl.

I know they won't find the airplane.

I read Sam a goodnight story, one ear listening for news from the next room. I love holding him in my lap, the way he snuggles in, his soft hair tickling my neck. He asks me many questions about hummingbirds, how they fly. He describes the beating of their wings, bats his eyes to demonstrate how fast. He describes Roger placing the bands, letting him touch the stunned birds. In his version, Roger is calm and in control and life is amazing. I want to freeze these moments for him before he succumbs to a world that is careening out of control. I want him to remember this, bonds this simple, this pure. I want to shield him from the sorrow in our home.

I wonder how Roger will live without Beth. Which will he miss more, the battles or the passionate lovemaking? The Jacuzzi in his backyard breaks my heart.

What is my mother thinking, asking to be present at the birth? How will she handle the mess of it all? The blood and gore of delivery? Will she need a drink? Will she and Sam stand together and watch as the midwives pull my baby into the world?

When I was a girl, my mother would play the radio while she cleaned the house "I am woman. Hear me roar." She would strut proudly across the living room pushing the vacuum like a bayonet. I never questioned what it took for my mother to be the primary wage earner in our family. I only held her accountable for her absences, her inability to "get" me. All the tools she offered me seemed wrong. The cherries she gave me from her manhattans were poisonous.

Now I am afraid of her flying. Afraid of having to reinvent her once again.

Very soon the hummingbirds will be gone. It's an endless cycle. It is an illusion that we can count on them returning. How can 245 people disappear into the Atlantic Ocean while a minute ruby throat makes its annual journey to Mexico unscathed? How can I dare to bring a child into this world and let my mother bear witness after fleeing from her in order to begin my life?

I feel a fluttering in my womb, already bracing for flight. Banded by me out of curiosity and a desire for evidence of my care. Will I have the chance to teach this child how to pick the fresh herbs from a summer garden? Will I have a chance to demonstrate to her how to preserve sustenance for the dark times? Will she be able to forgive me?

I warm water for tea and set out the peach cake on the kitchen table knowing it will offer little solace this dark night. Gestures are all we have. Food is as primal as we get. Sam is asleep with Skylar at his feet. The dog at the moment contentedly twitching as he runs through some dream field, young again. Roger has not set down his silent phone. We sit up all night, watching TV coverage, the endless loop of information that is not known, unable to turn off the anchor's morbid fascination. When the sun rises, we are already older.

As Roger pulls out of our driveway, I think: perhaps Skylar and I will wander the U-pick fields together before she dies. Maybe my mother will join us. When winter comes it will be too late. The dog's heart will give out. My mother will change her mind. Roger will be a widower with a white untanned ring around his finger.

But my freezer will be full. When winter buries the farm fields, the vegetables I have chopped will still be there, frozen or dried or packed in salt. During the darkest days, my pantry will overflow.

My farmers start planning spring crops in January. They draw maps and calculate demand. Like the flash of a ruby throat about to depart, the season is almost gone. Now is the time to prepare for the unforeseeable future.

D. Dina Friedman

When the Wind Ends

Through the window we watch the gliders settle,
dissolving into folded cloth on the field.
Their launching place—a break

in the treed-in ridgeline, where blazes end
on a flat rock; a green arrow pointing
to the edge—the leap

as fickle as funnel clouds
hurling homes. The lines
in our faces have slackened

into jowls. Our mouths betray
our bodies, which have shed their belief in wings.
As a child, you played Peter Pan,

broke your tooth bounding
from bedpost to bedpost. When we met,
there was something Never Neverland

in the way you walked, a springiness
under your arches, swaying hips
poised for take-off. It was all about wishes,

battered by the rush of air. You insist
you haven't grown wizened, only wiser,
but I'm still wooed by the scramble

to that green arrow edging over the cliff
the thrill of the forbidden jump
the widening of space.

Eileen P. Kennedy

Breakfast

September, your door ajar–
welcoming my mislaid soul,
a cup of coffee in hand,
in this many-windowed house
with the Steinway that holds the promise
of corresponding notes.
Your well-worn fingers on keys,
music midflight in your Rose of Sharon garden–
a minuet balancing the words on my keyboard.
This air still in our morning meeting
as if the world of care outside had stopped
to acknowledge our friendship.
How easily our union is fashioned
over scrambled eggs and hot-buttered toast.
I form an unseen poem around you
to seal our bond.

Marianne Gambaro

Transfiguration

Blackbirds shroud the flowering crab
in mourning.
Amid the squeaky rasp of starlings,
the rusty hinge screech of grackles,
and the mellifluous "o-kal-ree" of the redwings
an alien chirp.

Like the legendary emerald flash
above the sea as the sun gives in to night
a burst of green penetrates the shroud –
small feathered fugitive fleeing safety.
No coaxing can persuade him to give up
his ebony friends or new found freedom.

At daybreak a helicopter churns the air,
the percussion section of the blackbirds' symphony.
The police chief's robocall follows mid morning
Elderly Asian man missing from his home
in Lakes area since seventeen hundred
yesterday. Suffers from dementia.

In late afternoon searchers in close ranks
clad in Day-Glo vests invade suburban yards
kicking golden leaves, chatting
about baseball playoffs.

An abandoned chrysalis, his worn-out body
lies discarded in a nearby swamp
as his soul–flanked by a cacophony
of blackbirds–takes flight
in a rapturous emerald flash.

Maureen Solomon

One Afternoon

We were standing in the dark, brick lined room
while people dismantled the chairs all around us
an old friend and I getting our bearings after the
Remembrance Service.

You and I used to have wonderful conversations, he said
about life and what it means. His grey hair fell over his eyes
the way it always had. Was he waiting for me to say
something like what I might have said back then?

Instead he went on. *I have answered that question, I have solved
that problem. There is no meaning to life. You get to choose.
For yourself.* How quickly, I thought, this place for ceremony has been
dissolved. Tomorrow it will take another shape.

I didn't ask what he had chosen. Or tell him my own views.
Just now, I had already learned the meaning of life
for another friend, passed into what her son in his eulogy
called "The dancing place above us where everyone is nameless."

Instead I looked around the dim room. I like the idea of
that other place and of being without a name. Her history was
recited, her sorrows listed, her joys enumerated, now they
have drifted into these walls, into our hearts.

What we have each done is live. The living has been made by our selves.
Weaving good deeds with carelessness, love and parties,
books and tears, hours spent in drudgery, with money and without,
days in gardens, in misery. Another day, I may seek out this old friend.

I will want to see if the hair still falls into his eyes.

Lessons, Labyrinths, and Love Letters

D. Dina Friedman

Seven Lessons Learned from Sea Turtles

I.
The micromanaging mother is unnecessary.
It is enough to lay eggs in the sand
and trust the earth to hatch them.

II.
Keep walking; the sand is soft.
Eventually the ocean will pull you in.

III.
You can pretend to be a rock.
If you're lucky, no one will notice.
If not, bite.

IV.
The decoy nest, like the decoy word
fools only those who don't look deep.

V.
Learn to see in the dark.
Better yet, learn to compensate
for not being able to see in the dark.

VI.
Rejoice in your long life
the slow beauty of your aging.

VII.
Return to the places you love
even if you're not sure why you love them.

Jane McPhetres Johnson

Love Letter to My Neck

Ah, there you are, hanging out
under my chin, as usual. Rather
not as usual, exactly. You've loosened up
lately, lost your grip. Yet, you old
turkey wattle, I love you.

I buy you pretty scarves
and a new turtleneck
to hug you, neck and neck.
Okay, to hide you. But I can see

not wrinkles but reminders
that you have held my head
high in the face of hurt, that
you have allowed it to bow
in reverence, humility, loss.

That you have made possible
my head turning to satisfy
my heart and my natural bents.

I see this flabbiness
as flexibility: the give and
taking of a peek at the star
-studded treetops and into the tiniest
neighborhoods at my feet.

Well, that's a stretch
repeated and recorded
until your elastic's worn out.

Now you drag my redoubling
chin down with you and even replace
my rosy cheeks
with jowls. Still I will
love you, my good old neck,
for all these years you have made
way for head, body, and heart to
connec(k)t.

Maureen Solomon

When You Perceive Mortality

like red maple leaves in the sun,
it fills your eyes with purple curtains
then turns to dust

remember in Boston?
the trolleys took us to the ocean
in winter the boardwalk was shabby
an old naked woman waiting to die

there is a bridge over the creek
stand in the middle and watch the
water changing like the sky
violet and black and violet again

mud will run in your veins
but, if you could dream the hawk's flight path
it might not turn to ice

running won't help–just stop with your
foot in the air–dead oak leaves
make a perfect design on silver branches.

Eileen P. Kennedy

Here and Now

Abundant afternoon light
the heat of your shoulder
the secret of heliconia
the feel of your grace on my cheek
the mangoes rounded to the here and now.

We dance to Ella Fitzgerald
you: lost in the trance
of her discordant strain
me: in your arms
totally here, now.

Let's tango into older age
grounded by earth and limb.
Our bodies ram shackled,
still able to toddle across the floor,
clumsy, out of step.

Let's be insatiable you and I.
Not gently, but raging forward
bowin', swayin',
dippin', cavortin', and struttin'
into the here and now.

Epi Bodhi

The Ring

I always wanted my mother's wedding band
It was nothing pretentious
But it was her
In her youth and in her old age
All wrapped up in her hands

Years ago, after I had breast cancer
She gave me the ring
Said it was to keep me safe
Then she took it back

Maybe she needed it to keep her safe
In her new New Jersey life

Told me I could have it after she died

In her befuddlement, the ring was lost
Packing up her apartment, we all looked for it
But
It was lost

Five days after she died
Four of us sorted through her storage unit
Read through old cards and papers
Looked at her house dresses
With fond memories and great sadness

I was drawn to her purse
Her last purse
That came places with her when
She no longer needed a purse

I don't know why I wanted it
Isn't my style
But still I took it And used it

Naima helped me load it
We found folded tissues,
A wallet with a few photos, a driver's license hardly used,
Two rain bonnets neatly folded in their cases
And a small turquoise ring

I wear the ring,
Carry the purse
I can take the grief
In these small bits

Tonight
Not for the first time
I reached into the purse for my office keys
Pulled out my hand and there was the ring

I'm trying to make sense of it
But I can't
Clearly it was meant to be
The lost ring
The purse

My mother gives presents from the world beyond.

Eileen P. Kennedy

rainbow

heliconia space and grace
crimson sundown paddling
father's inflamed legs
lipstick on white tissue
night hospital sore eyes

costa rican market fruit
monarch butterfly there as well
father's auburn waning hair
ginger and carrot on green salad
fishing catch bobber floating

savory corn butter bliss
honey garland passion dew
sail across father's boat
copper-lit manhattan building
beigy bhudda's belly luck rub

spiraled sapphire water
fountain pen stain
pain circling hazel-eyed father
cobalt colleague's card
cerulean verses almost like the blues

avocado split to the center
jade necklace gift
chemo pale father's hand
emerald earth-lit hills
another promotion envy

pope's violet robe
lavender buds in bath
father's breathless face
lilacs' spring perfume
mauve bishop's blessing over heads

i dance many-hued dahlias in my hair
color energy on fire
no metaphor can bring my father back

D. Dina Friedman

Where I Am From

I am from buildings and concrete, from subways lined with spit,
from dark lights, thick letters announcing untaken exits.

I am from dirt, the dying sand under backyard sidewalks
where carrot tops killed for surface space in the one available crack.

I am from weeds, and the miracle of bulbs
returning to their place of birth. I am from ink, spilling and spilt,

then bursting, like businessmen swarming out of subways.
I am from dinner parties and dirty plates,

from the shades pulled in the living room
where my great grandmother sat in her black chair peeking out

between soiled Venetian blinds as I emerged
from a powder blue dress, its starched skirt twirling

under its own steam
like a 50s dream.

Jane McPhetres Johnson

His Long Fingers Moved

like small animals through
grasslands to explore my
scalp, lifting thick hair as
casually as an old lover
then searched my face
touching temple, cheek
brow but oh so carefully
brushing my skin with his
fingertips, never allowing
eyes to meet eyes but
taking it all in and then
my neck and slipping off
the gown to bare shoulders
gazing down the length of
one arm after the other at
tender inner skin creases
and freckles, spots and
scars, reading the map of
my life, giving all of me such
tender and rare attention
turning from breasts to
spine, hips to thighs and
even every single toe until
he was intimately familiar
with every inch of my skin
nothing under or within: so
chary my deft dermatologist.

Epi Bodhi

The Subway Ride

The subway traveled from Coney Island through Manhattan to the Bronx, its gray body on tracks overhead and underground picking up and depositing people along the way. A cleverer person could have analyzed the class and migration structure of the City.

My stop was close to the beginning where poverty and foreign tongues gave way to second-generation middle classness. A small enclave of private homes and tiny yards where people boarding the train carried newspapers and attractive handbags, wore suits and fur coats (sometimes turned inwards to avoid attention). They spoke in subdued tones but remained alert.

At Prospect Park station, all those who entered were dark-skinned, carried bag lunches, spoke louder. I thought they belonged to a club that I wanted to join.

All the seats filled up as we went underground towards downtown Brooklyn. Sometimes my mother and I got off here, in downtown, to do our shopping at the "Department Stores"- Mays for bargains and A&S for class. Those were not my favorite times.

I preferred continuing on when the subway reemerged into the air and onto the bridge where I could stand up and see our lady all in green with her raised torch welcoming the huddled masses. I felt it was my duty to stand up and watch her as we passed.

Further on, back underground, at Grand Street, all the people entering became Asian, spoke quickly, filled the car with the yummy smells of our restaurant meals.

Infrequently, brown skinned people, also speaking a tongue I did not understand, entered and exited the train. I withdrew from them, thought them dirty. Where and how does a child pick up these things? I'm sure nothing explicit was ever said.

I remember, my parents correcting my grandfather when he spoke of "schwartzer" which could sometimes be translated as "nigger". I remember too, my mother serving Ida, the large Black Woman who came once or twice a week to clean our house and do the ironing, a lunch of hot dogs and tea. They treated each other with respect. Though my mother, also Ida, was Mrs. Epton while Ida remained Ida and received what my mother gave her for food, pay and bus fare.

Somehow, I knew it was wrong and my mother knew it was wrong and transmitted to me the unfairness of how the "Negroes" were treated in our country.

Asian people were exotic, had their own culture, which was to be respected, made great food, ran the laundry where we took my father's shirts to be pressed once a week.

But this thing about Brown people where did that come from?

The Avenue, where we shopped closer to home was like this as well. Small shops each with their known but undeclared nationality; the Italian fish monger, the Jewish butcher and vegetable stand, the Chinese laundry where we took my father's shirts and communicated with few words and hand gestures, Mike the Italian shoe repair man, who touched my little sister inappropriately and she was told to ignore it.

Marianne Gambaro

The Labyrinth at Kripalu

It is September. Horse chestnuts, like those collected by my father on the day I was born, stud the pathway to the labyrinth at the yoga center. My mother had been in labor for three days and he, feeling useless and wearied by watching her efforts and by my recalcitrance, had gone for a walk. In the hospital parking lot he picked up several horse chestnuts that lay scattered on the asphalt in the shadow of their parent tree; that tree had no doubt given birth much more easily than what my mother was enduring.

Each year my father gave me a handful of horse chestnuts on my birthday until he could no longer find the tree. Or, being a man who held his emotions close, perhaps he decided that I was too old for such sentimentality.

Tibetan prayer flags frame the entry to the labyrinth, fraying their intentions heavenward to the supreme power of choice. Blue tiles and granite cobblestones define the path punctuated by diligently pruned conifers. An errant branch juts out in defiance from an otherwise perfectly manicured hemlock.

One year, away at college on my birthday, I sent my father a cigarillo box filled with horse chestnuts. He never acknowledged my reverse gift. I assumed he thought the postage was a frivolous expense for a student on a budget.

The center of the labyrinth—the goal – is always in sight. It would be so easy to cross the low tiles to reach it. So easy to cheat–but why? Isn't the real goal in fact the journey to find my own center? Like that tired old yoga joke: Yogi to hot dog vendor: "Make me one with everything." Hands the vendor a twenty-dollar bill and looks at him expectantly waiting for his change. Vendor to yogi: "Change comes from within."

Five decades after my birth it was I who stood at his hospital beds–through bypass surgery, eight years of dialysis, and other ailments that assaulted his once strong body. After he died I found that cigarillo box with the horse chestnuts and my note in his nightstand as I was emptying out the house where he and my mother had lived for more than half a century. I threw away the note but the box still sits on my desk.

To find the center let go thoughts and distractions: reflect, meditate, realign, open the mind, tolerate, forgive, accept. To find truth find meaning; to find meaning find truth.

Just as the center seems within reach the path leads teasingly back to the outermost edge. *Be open. Be flexible. Embrace change.* I find the labyrinth comforting because, unlike life, there is only one path to follow, no choices to be made – one less distraction, one less burden.

Finally I come to the center. It is cluttered – no, littered – with tributes to... whom or what? A glass bear. A piece of brain coral. Notes scribbled on scraps of paper, even on candy wrappers. And the ubiquitous, valueless pennies. Bet they weren't much of a sacrifice.

I reach into my jacket and pants pockets looking for a tribute and come up empty. Certainly a dirty Kleenex won't do. And I'll need my car keys to get back to the real world. I have no part of me to leave here and wonder why I've come after all.

Turning away I see, half hidden beneath a hemlock, a broken green hull still cradling its charge. My offering. Reverently I place my tribute in the heart of the labyrinth as I whisper my father's name and think of the young man who, so many years ago, picked up horse chestnuts in a hospital parking lot while his wife struggled to give me life.

And I begin the journey back out of the labyrinth to find the tree.

Maureen Solomon

Sisters at the Carnival

Memory captures us pinned on
top of the roller coaster in Billings—
we hang on in dizzy hysteria
poised for descent into magic prairie,
dusty sprawl of blurry faces and glitter.

Do you remember how the ride ends
with that feeling of something emptied
from the entire universe, those wooden bottles
nailed to the floor, how you save your dimes
and I lose all mine, victim of giddy greed,

how we stick our tongues into cotton candy
melting in our hair? Your hands are gritty,
sweat holds us together behind the fortune teller
where Aunt Helen has disappeared into popcorn air,
in manure scented evening we are lost,

cut loose, miasma of danger all around,
filled with dark exhilaration, with syrupy breath,
fear and happiness like giant purple balloons
lift us along the crowded midway.
Can you ever hear the carnival organ
without feeling that wild fierce joy?

Jane McPhetres Johnson

There's a Term for That

when one's body remembers
an earlier evolutionary state
when for example my milk
came in soon after you my son
and fulfilled finally my girlish
dreams of a fullness to fill
my hitherto boyish hope chest
but then surprise! Your appetite
called for more and found it
under one arm, with no nipple
for relief, explained the nurse
binding it tightly, an anomaly
a throwback beyond ancestors
maybe a myth like a wolf with
enough nipples to serve the
whole sucking litter all at once.
My body knew better of course
in due time planting new growth
unwelcome comeback cruel joke
where a third nipple should have
been but even so I feel this odd
connection with that ominous
fairytale grandmother who left me
this tender anomalous gift from her
long ago abundance of breasts.

About the Contributors

Epi Bodhi has been writing poetry since she was young. In the third grade, she was accused of plagiarism for her poem *snowflake*. She has spent many years in the field of Public Health both locally and internationally. As part of the Friday morning cohousing writing group she has rediscovered her passion for writing, particularly memoir poems.

D. Dina Friedman has received two Pushcart Prize nominations and published in many journals including *Calyx, Negative Capability, San Pedro River Review, Bloodroot, Inkwell, Tsunami, The Sun, Anderbo,* and *Rhino*. Dina is also the author of two award-winning young adult novels, **Escaping Into the Night** (Simon and Schuster) and **Playing Dad's Song** (Farrar, Straus, Giroux). She has an MFA from Lesley University and teaches at the University of Massachusetts/ Amherst. Visit her website at http://www.ddinafriedman.com.

Marianne Gambaro's poems have been published in several print and online journals including *The Aurorean, Oberlin Poetry Magazine, Pirene's Fountain, Avocet Journal, Snowy Egret* and *The Naugatuck River Review*. Her upcoming chapbook, **Do NOT Stop for Hitchhikers**, will be published in early 2018 by Finishing Line Press. Following a career as a journalist and public relations practitioner for nonprofit organizations, she now writes for the sheer love of the word. She is a member of the Florence (MA) Poets Society and serves on the editorial team for *Silkworm*, their annual journal. She resides in verdant Western Massachusetts, with her talented photographer-husband and three feline muses.

Kathryn Holzman attended Stanford and NYU. While in NYC, she co-ran Backroom Readings and had poetry published in the US & Hong Kong before pursuing a career in Healthcare Administration. Now residing in New England with her husband, a digital artist, she has had short stories published in *The Adirondack Review, Atticus Review, Map Literary, Cowboy Jamboree* and *the Fictional Cafe* and is currently working on a novel set in Silicon Valley. Read more of her short stories in her chapbook, **Migrations**, available at http://picaflorpress.weebly.com.

Jane McPhetres Johnson completed an MFA from Goddard College in VT the same year the writing program moved to Warren Wilson in NC and the same week her younger son Ben Johnson (with an "h") was born. At the time, Jane was living in northern Wyoming and commuting to Vermont for biannual residencies while doing some work as a Poet in the Schools and teaching at the local college. Eventually she moved east and began working for the New England Foundation for the Humanities, creating and coordinating literature and history programs in public libraries, recently moving to Amherst, where she is haunted by Emily Dickinson and walks almost daily on the Robert Frost trail, finally picking up where she left off when life barged in.

Eileen P. Kennedy's BANSHEES (Flutter Press, 2015) was nominated for a Pushcart Prize in 2016 and awarded Second Prize from the Wordwrite Book Awards in Poetry. She won Honorable Mention from the New England, New York and London Book Festivals, as well as from the Tom Howard/Margaret Reid/Poetry Contest and the Oregon Poetry Society. She has published poetry in more than 25 literary journals. She has also published a textbook, fiction and nonfiction. She has been awarded residences at the Woodstock Byrdcliffe Guild, Woodstock, NY, AIR 'Le Parc,' Pampellonne, France, and the Hambidge Center for Creative Arts, Rabun Gap, Georgia. She holds a doctorate in language and literacy and has been a faculty member of the City University of New York. She lives in Amherst, MA. More at EileenPKennedy.com.

Maureen Solomon is a poet, potter, photographer and painter. She lives in the country with her husband, Richard, and plants flowers wherever she can find a place for them. She is a member of the Wednesday Afternoon Poets in Monson, MA and the Florence Poets Society.

Acknowledgments

Many thanks to the editors and journals who published many of these poems and stories.

The Lupines of Ushuaia, by Marianne Gambaro: Published in *Avocet, A Journal of Nature Poems*, Winter 2011

Consider the Turnip, by D. Dina Friedman: Published in *Anderbo*, March 2010

I Don't Know What the Wooly Bear Knows, by Maureen Solomon: Published in *Silkworm 7*, 2014

Spring Song, by Eileen P. Kennedy: Published in *Silkworm 9*, 2016

Last Light Rondeau, by Marianne Gambaro: Published in *Snowy Egret*, Spring/Autumn 2015

Some Day, by D. Dina Friedman: Published in *Indiana Voice Journal*, March 2015

Summer Reunion, **Breakfast**, and **Here and Now** by Eileen P. Kennedy: Published in **Banshees** Flutter Press, 2015

Dog Days by Kathryn Holzman: Published in *JunoEsq*, Singapore, 2015

When the Wind Ends, by D. Dina Friedman: Published in *Xanadu*, 2016

Transfiguration, by Marianne Gambaro: Published in *Pirene's Fountain*, April 2015

Seven Lessons Learned from Sea Turtles, by D. Dina Friedman: Published in *Mount Hope*, Fall 2012

rainbow, by Eileen P. Kennedy: Published in *Oberon*, 2016

Where I Am From, by D. Dina Friedman: Published in *Red Booth Review*, December 2012

The Labyrinth at Kripalu, by Marianne Gambaro: Published in *Touch*: *The Journal of Healing*, Autumn 2013

www.ingramcontent.com/pod-product-compliance
Lightning Source LLC
Chambersburg PA
CBHW031904170626
46807CB00004B/1884